SUPER SMART INFORMATION STRATEGIES

WRITE IT DOWN

by Julie Green

CHERRY LAKE PUBLISHING • ANN ARBOR, MICHIGAN

A NOTE TO PARENTS AND TEACHERS: Please remind your children how to stay safe online before they do the activities in this book.

A NOTE TO KIDS: Always remember your safety comes first!

CHERRY LAKE Publishing

Published in the United States of America
by Cherry Lake Publishing
Ann Arbor, Michigan
www.cherrylakepublishing.com

Content Adviser: Gail Dickinson, PhD,
Associate Professor, Old Dominion University,
Norfolk, Virginia

Book design and illustration: The Design Lab

Photo credits: Cover, ©Sabphoto/Dreamstime.com; pages 3, 6, 7, 9 right, 11, 12 left, 12 right, 19, 27, and 29, ©iStockphoto.com/bluestocking; page 4, ©Supri Suharjoto, used under license from Shutterstock, Inc.; page 9 left, ©iStockphoto.com/RapidEye; page 13, ©Lisafx/Dreamstime.com; page 15, ©Mikdam/Dreamstime.com; page 22, ©Duckpondstudios/Dreamstime.com

Library of Congress Cataloging-in-Publication Data
Green, Julie, 1982–
Super smart information strategies: write it down / by Julie Green.
p. cm.—(Information explorer)
Includes bibliographical references and index.
ISBN-13: 978-1-60279-645-4 (lib.bdg.)
ISBN-13: 978-1-61080-266-6 (pbk.)
1. Note-taking—Juvenile literature. I. Title. II. Series.
LB2395.25.G74 2010
371.3028'1—dc22
2009024741

Cherry Lake Publishing would like to acknowledge the work of The Partnership for 21st Century Skills. Please visit *www.21stcenturyskills.org* for more information.

Printed in the United States of America
Corporate Graphics Inc.
December 2011
CLFA09

Table of Contents

Chapter One: Highlighting

CHAPTER ONE

Highlighting

Imagine sitting at your desk during social studies class. You have just finished doing a group activity when your teacher says, "And for homework tonight, read chapter three and take notes." You silently groan to yourself. "Taking notes" has never been very clear to you. How do you do it? Why do you have to take notes and who even does that outside of school? What is note taking anyway?

Don't just think about it—put your pencil to the paper and take some notes!

Note taking is the process of collecting important information and organizing it in a way that is helpful for you to use later. Note taking can be done in very different ways by different people. Scientists take notes when they observe experiments. Friends might take notes when planning what to bring to the pool party next Saturday. A waitress takes notes when she asks you what you'd like to order for dinner at a restaurant. All of these people take notes to help them remember or understand something. But their notes will probably be in very different forms. The important thing to remember is that note taking is a very personal activity. You have to use the method that works best for you. Let's look at some of those methods.

Waiters and waitresses have a secret for remembering your food order. They take notes!

Consider THIS

Evaluating your sources and the information they contain is very important. What's the point of taking notes if the information is not accurate or does not relate to your topic? Ask yourself these questions about a source to determine if it is something you should use. When was the book or article published? If it is very old, you may not want to use it. Who wrote this source? Does this person seem like an expert on the subject? Is she presenting the topic in a fair manner? Be extra careful with online sources. Who published the Web site? Is it an organization you can trust to give accurate facts? When was the site updated? Taking the time to evaluate information and find reliable sources will help you be successful in school!

A space travel book from 1963 is not a good source for current information about outer space.

Taking notes is kind of like making a sandwich. First, you have to gather the bread and different ingredients to put between the slices. Then you can arrange them to make a delicious snack. When taking notes, you have to gather the information first. Then you can put it together in a way that makes sense to you.

Highlighting is one very popular way to gather information. A highlighter is a special kind of marker. Its ink is a lighter color than a regular marker's. The text you highlight can still be easily read. While reading an article or book, you might find a phrase that seems important. You can use a highlighter to mark those words so they stand out. It can be difficult to figure out what is important enough to highlight and what can be left alone. How much highlighting is too much? If the text is completely covered with highlighter ink by the time you've finished reading, that's too much!

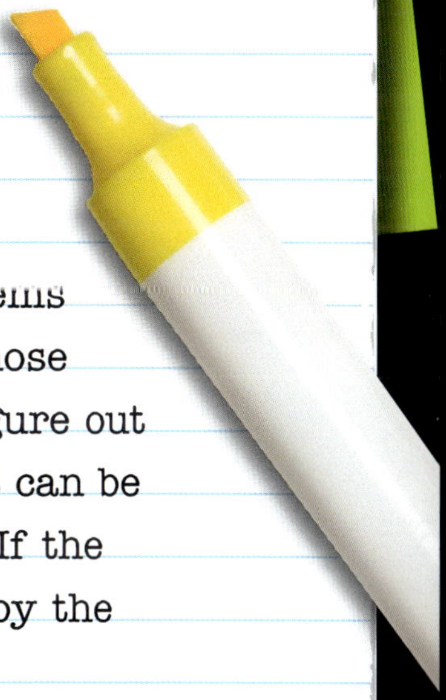

Highlighting should help you pick out the main ideas of an article. You should be able to quickly glance at what you've highlighted and understand the main points. Try reading the headings of a chapter or section of text. Headings explain the main idea of a paragraph. They give you a hint about what it's all about. Do your best to make sure everything you highlight relates back to that heading. Pay special attention to topic sentences, bold print, and the first and last paragraphs. These areas might give you clues about main ideas.

Another helpful tip is to read the article once through without highlighting anything. Try to get the main idea. Then go back and read it more carefully, highlighter in hand. Only highlight what seems to be the main idea of the article. You might like using highlighters of different colors to organize your information. Picture an article about Revolutionary War heroes. You might use a pink highlighter for important dates and a green one for essential people. Then when you go back to the article later, you'll be able to spot different types of information. The best way to get used to the process is to practice.

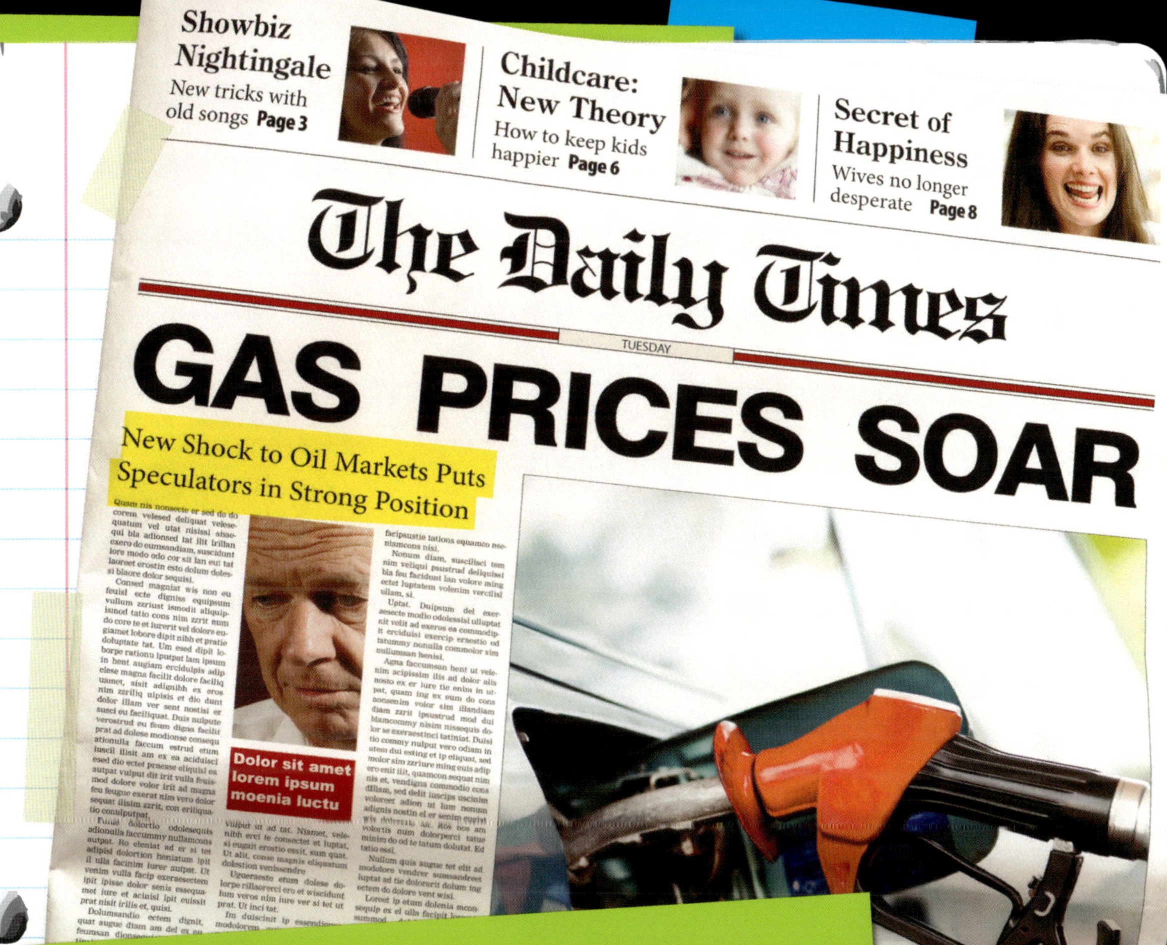

TRY THIS!

Grab a highlighter. Pick a magazine or print out an online article that you find interesting and have permission to highlight. Look for the title, headings, bold print, and first and last paragraphs. Looking at these sections will help you understand what the article is about. Then go back and read through the entire text. Begin to highlight important points. When you're finished, pretend that you're someone who has never read this article. If that person read only what you've highlighted, would she understand the main ideas? If the answer is yes, pat yourself on the back. Then grab another article and practice again!

Chapter Two: Using Sticky Notes

CHAPTER TWO

Using Sticky Notes

Another way to take notes is with the help of sticky notes. You might use large sticky notes to write down many thoughts. Or you might choose small skinny ones to stick on the edge of a page, marking it as an important section. Pick the kind of sticky note that works best for you.

The process of determining what information is most important when using sticky notes is pretty much the same as with highlighting. Read the headings and

Sticky notes come in all different sizes and colors.

bold print. Figure out the main ideas. The sticky notes will allow you to add your own thoughts and questions. Let's pretend you're reading an article about the best ice cream shops in your area. You read that a certain shop has "the best vanilla ice cream in town." You really like vanilla ice cream so you want to remember this parlor. But your all-time favorite is chocolate chip cookie dough. So, you take one of your sticky notes and place it right next to the spot in the article that mentions that parlor. On the sticky note you write, "Best vanilla! Do they have chocolate chip cookie dough? Call and ask." The next time you look at this article, your eye will go right to the place that serves the best vanilla ice cream. But you'll also remember that you should call ahead if you're in the mood for chocolate chip cookie dough.

Writing things down can help your brain remember information. After all, taking notes requires you to think and focus on determining what information is important enough to jot down. Reading helps you gather a lot of information. But sometimes that information leads to more questions. Sticky notes give you a place to record the questions you have. As you continue to read, you might think, "Hey! Here's the answer to my question from an earlier chapter." You can easily go back to your previous sticky note and write in the answer.

Sticky notes also give you the option of organizing information by color. Choose one color of sticky notes for questions. Choose a different color for important facts.

Consider this . . .

If you don't have sticky notes, you can try another option. Use different colored pens or pencils and write in the margins of the text. You can even circle words you don't know and look them up later. Just make sure you have permission to write in the source you are using!

TRY THIS!

It's time for a trip to the library. Check out a nonfiction book about an insect of your choice. Army ants or praying mantises are just two options. You'll need some sticky notes and a pencil. Then follow the steps on the following page.

(continued on page 14)

TRY THIS! (CONTINUED)

1. Look at the title of the first chapter and begin reading.
2. As you read, place sticky notes along the margins of important sections. Write anything that comes to mind on the notes. You can jot down guesses about what might be discussed later in the book. You can also note what you think about the main ideas or questions you have about some of the facts.
3. After you've finished reading the book, go back and look at your sticky notes. Pay special attention to the ones from that first chapter. Were your predictions correct? Did your questions get answered? Do you see how sticky notes can help organize your thoughts?

All those sticky notes will help you find information quickly when you need it.

CHAPTER THREE

Tables

Highlighters and sticky notes are great tools. They allow you to pick out important information when reading something. Sometimes, however, you are asked to find very specific information.

Pretend that your class is studying types of transportation. Your teacher puts you in a group of five students. Each of you is in charge of researching one of the following ways to travel: train, car, bus, airplane, or horse-drawn carriage. You have to research and become an expert on trains. Then you need to return to your group and teach the others about them. Where do

How fast do trains move? Take a guess and check your answer on page 17.

you start? Luckily, your teacher has given you a list of things you must learn about trains. You already know what you need to look for. So a table might be a great way for you to take notes. Tables use columns and rows to help organize the information.

At the top of your table, you will write a heading for each column. In the left-hand column, you will list the points about trains that your teacher assigned you to research. You can list these points in the form of a question. The center column is for information you find as you read. You might also want to add a right-hand column that asks a certain question. This question can help you think about the information you find in a special way. It helps you make connections to other information and ideas.

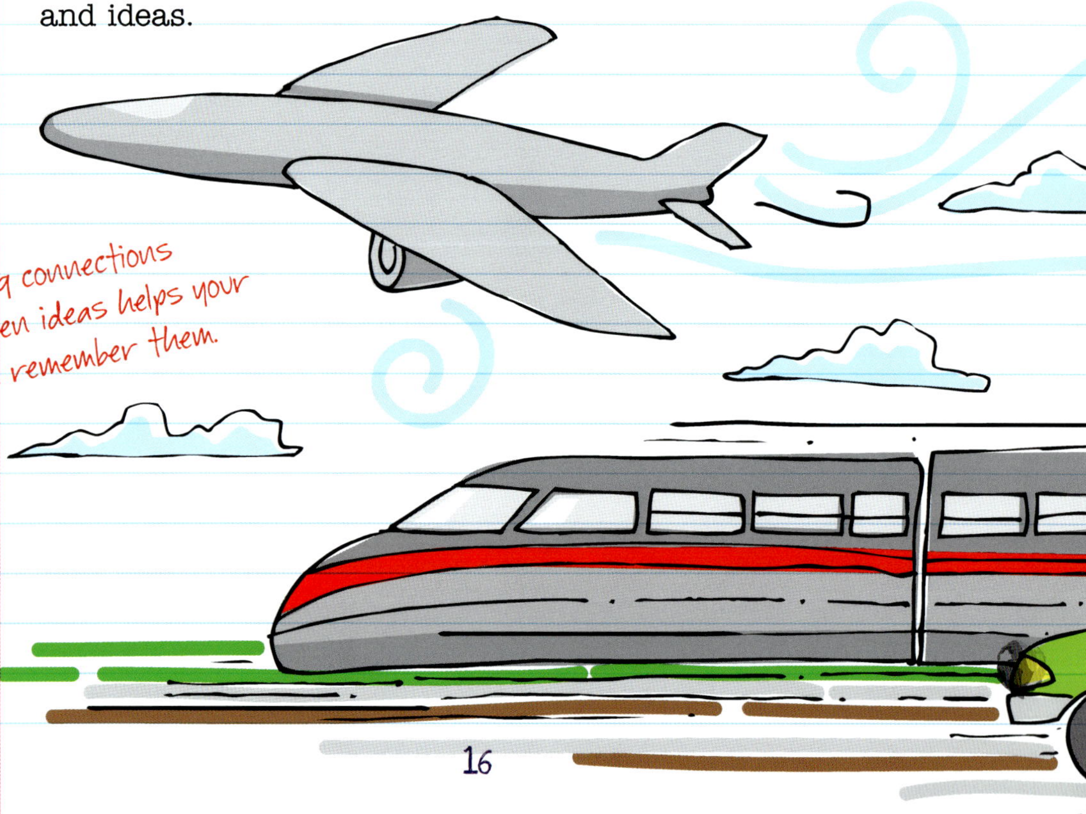

Making connections between ideas helps your brain remember them.

Here is an example of a table for your project on trains:

Trains

Question	Information I Found	How does the information I found compare to cars, buses, airplanes, or horse-drawn carriages?
How fast can trains go?	Some can go faster than 200 miles (321.9 kilometers) per hour	Faster than horse-drawn carriages, buses, and most cars; slower than planes
Who might use trains?	Travelers, companies transporting goods	Same groups often use cars, buses, and airplanes; horse-drawn carriages are probably used for different reasons, such as tourism
When were trains invented?	First locomotives developed in early 1800s	After horse-drawn carriages, but before cars, buses, and planes
Are there different kinds of trains?	Yes: passenger trains, locomotives, freight trains, and more	There are different kinds of all of these forms of transportation

Did you Know this?

Always remember to give credit to the source where you found your facts. This is called citing your information. If you find useful facts for your trains project in a book, you should cite the book. See the card below to find out how.

A CITATION LOOKS LIKE THIS:

Marsico, Katie. *Trains*. Ann Arbor, MI: Cherry Lake Publishing, 2009.

Put the title of the book in italic.

Remember to include this information in your citation:

- AUTHOR'S NAME: Katie Marsico
- BOOK TITLE: Trains
- CITY OF PUBLICATION: Ann Arbor
- PUBLISHER'S NAME: Cherry Lake Publishing
- DATE OF PUBLICATION: 2009

Web sites, books, and other sources are all cited in different ways. Your teacher or a librarian will be happy to help you figure out how to cite a source. When in doubt, just ask!

There might be assignments in which no one has given you specific information to find. Could you still use a table to take notes? Yes! In this case, you can easily make a two-column table. First, take a piece of paper and fold it in half lengthwise. In the left-hand column, write "Important Topics or Ideas." In the right-hand column, write "Facts and Details." Remember to write down only the most important pieces of information in the right-hand column. You don't want to get in the habit of writing everything down. You won't find your notes very helpful. Plus, your hand will get tired!

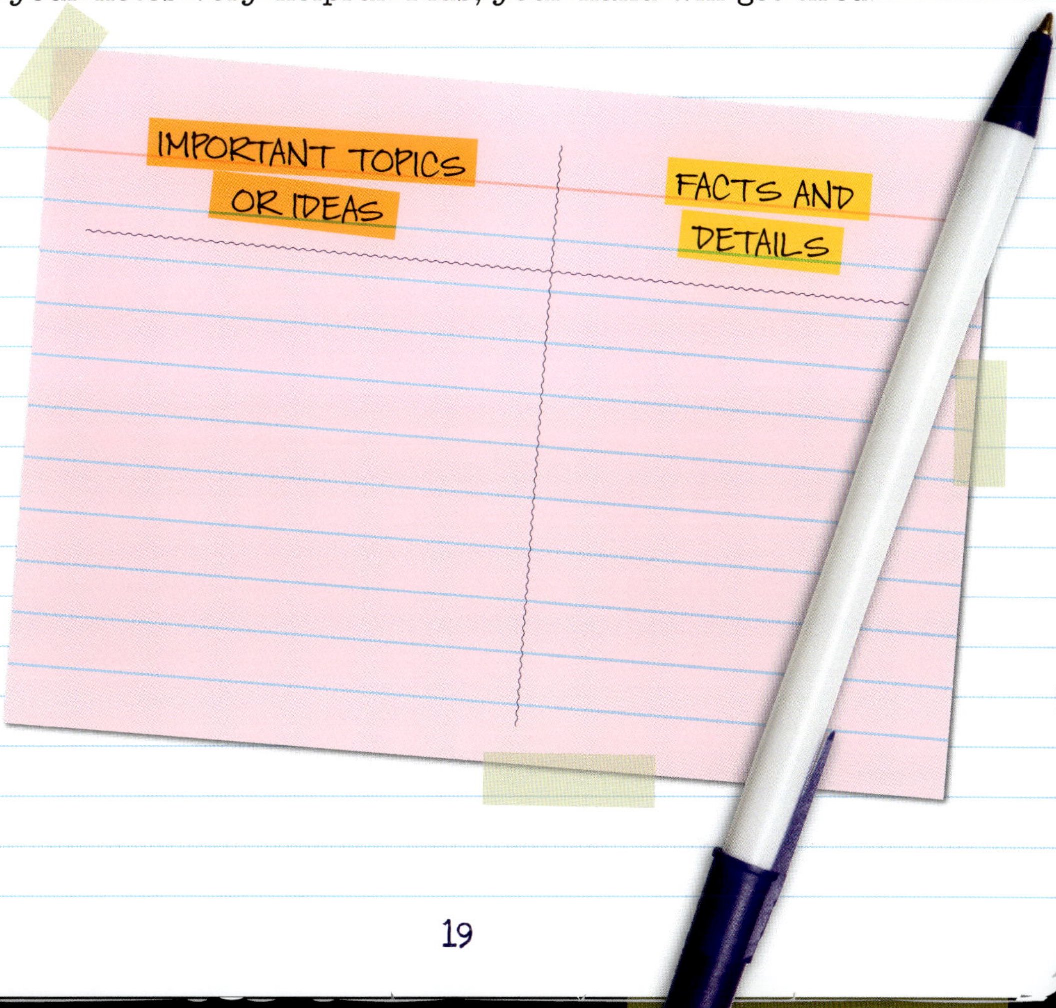

TRY THIS!

Choose a country that you would like to visit. Can't think of one? How about Japan, Brazil, or Libya? Use a reliable source, such as an encyclopedia article, to fill in the following table. Ask your teacher or a librarian if you need help tracking down other reliable sources.

Stop, don't write in the book!

A country I would like to visit

Question	Information I Found	How does the information I found differ from facts about my own country?
What kind of foods do the people eat?		
What are some favorite things for people to do in their free time?		
What languages do the people speak?		
What are some of the country's major landforms?		

Chapter Three: Tables

Tables are one kind of graphic organizer. Graphic organizers arrange information in visual ways. This can make it easier for people to understand relationships, differences, and patterns between pieces of information. There are many types of graphic organizers. These include flow charts and time lines.

A family tree is a type of flow chart.

CHAPTER FOUR

Visual Note Taking

A map can be a helpful tool when taking notes.

By now, you know that there are several ways to take notes using written words. These methods can be very useful. But sometimes words are just not enough. Tables and charts give us a glimpse of how arranging information in visual ways can help us organize notes. But you might also find it helpful to draw a picture, make a flow chart, or create a map. Flow charts often use boxes and arrows. They show the step-by-step order of an event or process. Creating visual representations such as these can be great learning tools. You can add these representations to your written notes. Or you can replace written words with sketches. With time, you'll discover what works best for you.

Maybe you are planning a trip around the state of Michigan. You want to see some of the waterfalls in the area. You can do more than just write out a list of places. You could plot and label them on a map of the state. Now when you look at the map, you can figure out many things. You can see how many waterfalls you are interested in visiting and how far away they are from one another.

Visual note taking can be extra helpful for certain subjects in school. Think about the water cycle. Simply reading about the process of the water cycle might be confusing. Wouldn't creating a chart or map of the stages of the cycle help clear things up? A chart with a few images, short phrases, and arrows could help you picture the process. Who knew you could get so creative with your note taking?

TRY THIS!

Think about an average Monday in your life. Use some kind of visual representation to map out the events of your day. Start with when you wake up. Keep going until bedtime. You can use a diagram, flow chart, or whatever you feel best explains your day. How about using a time line? You can note the times of different events in your day. Then you can use words and pictures to describe the events. You could make your own time line. Or you could find a blank one online, print it out, and then fill in the spaces. Look over your time line or visual representation when you finish. You may just find that your "average" Monday wasn't so average after all.

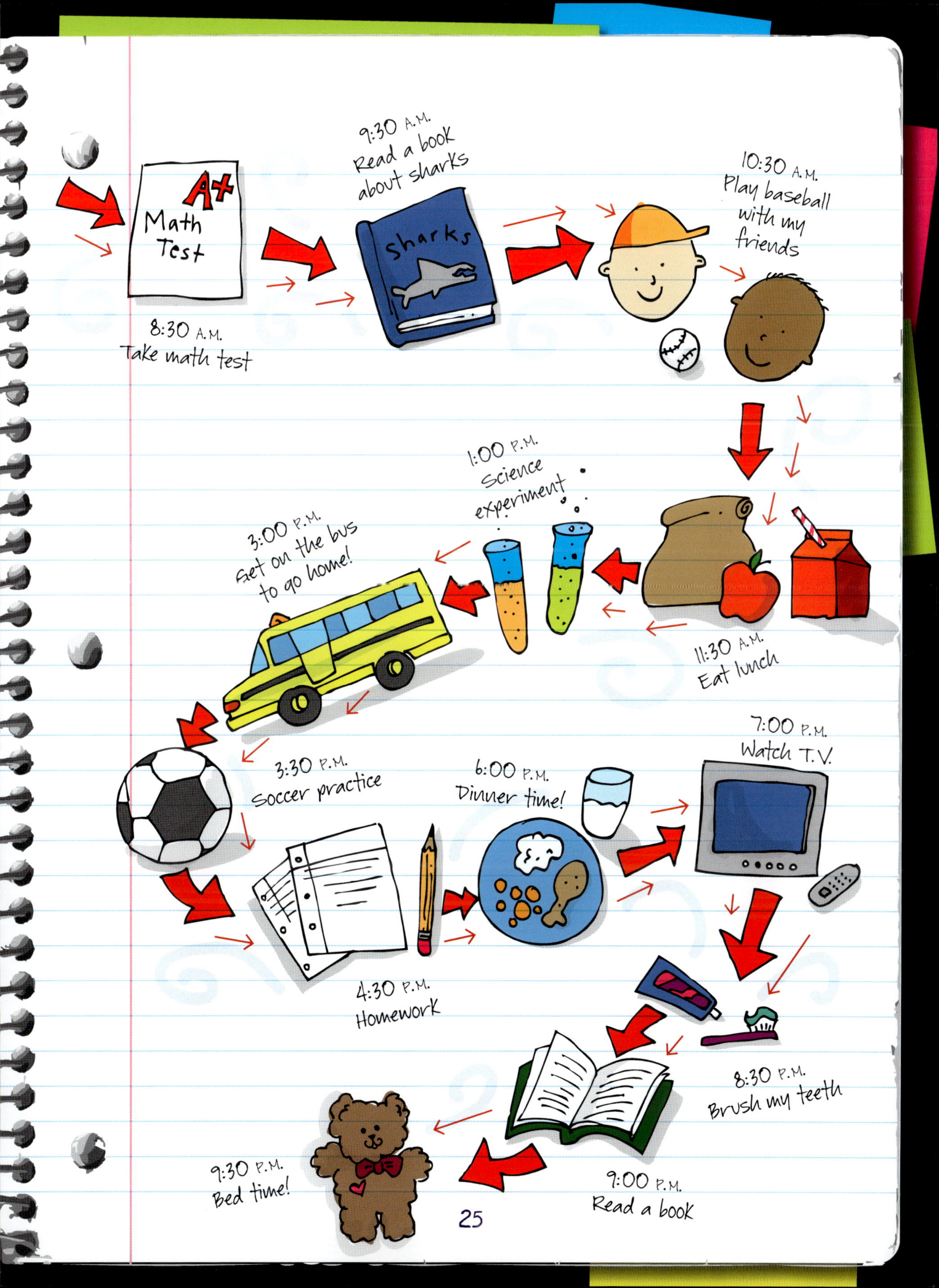

A+
Math Test
8:30 A.M.
Take math test
Sharks
9:30 A.M.
Read a book about sharks
10:30 A.M.
Play baseball with my friends
11:30 A.M.
Eat lunch
1:00 P.M.
Science experiment
3:00 P.M.
Get on the bus to go home!
3:30 P.M.
Soccer practice
4:30 P.M.
Homework
6:00 P.M.
Dinner time!
7:00 P.M.
Watch T.V.
8:30 P.M.
Brush my teeth
9:00 P.M.
Read a book
9:30 P.M.
Bed time!

CHAPTER FIVE

Venn Diagrams

Taking notes isn't always about finding information on a single topic. Many times you will be looking for information about two different subjects. Or you may have to investigate two sides of an idea. This type of research can help you better understand a topic.

Consider THIS

Part of being a responsible note taker means putting information in your own words. The idea sounds simple. But, along with citing your sources, it is very important. You do not want to copy an idea word for word from a source. You might make the mistake of including those word-for-word notes in an essay, project, or report. You could get into a lot of trouble—whether or not it was an accident.

Let's pretend you and a friend are researching two different kinds of fruit. You researched raspberries. Your friend researched cherries. You know the two fruits are similar in some ways. But you also know that they are very different. To discover more about these fruits, you can use a Venn diagram. A Venn diagram is another kind of graphic organizer. It has two circles that overlap. In one circle, you will put all of the details that relate only to cherries. In the other circle, you will put all of the details that relate only to raspberries. Where the two circles overlap, you will write all of the facts that relate to both kinds of fruit. Here is a simple version of what your diagram might look like:

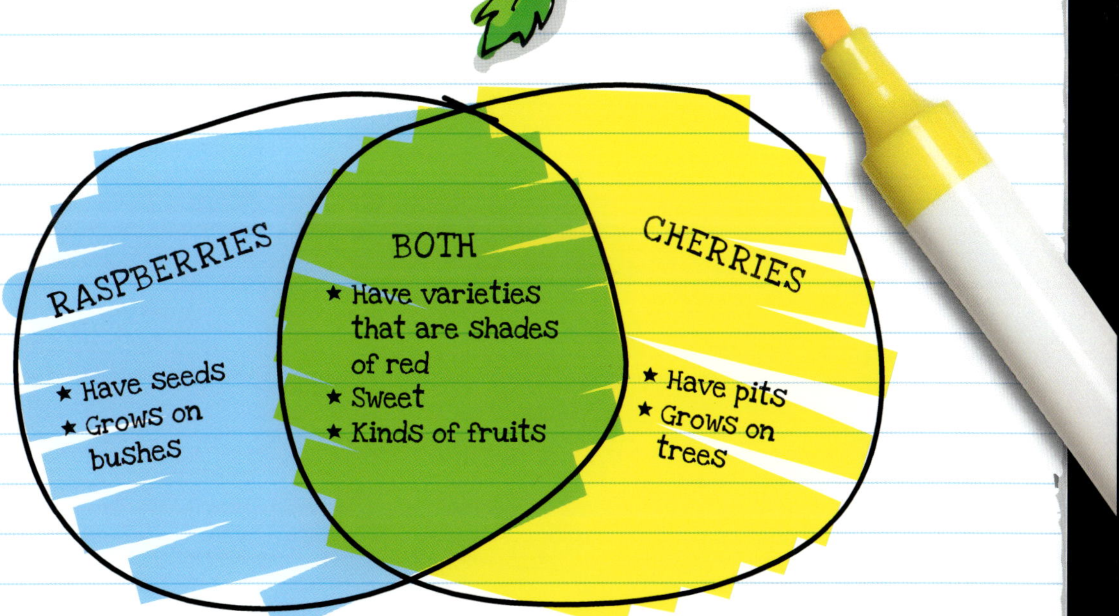

Are you a fan of graphic organizers? Ask an adult to help you find more types online.

A Venn diagram can let you see what is similar and what is different about two subjects. You might use a Venn diagram to organize notes that you've already taken. Arranging your information in the diagram can help give you a new understanding of the ideas. You are sorting the facts in a fresh way.

TRY THIS!

It's time to make your own Venn diagram.

1. Think about your two favorite things to do during summer vacation.
2. In the left-hand circle of your diagram, write down everything that relates only to Favorite Activity #1.
3. In the right-hand circle, write down only what relates to Favorite Activity #2.
4. In the overlapping section, write down everything you can think of that relates to both activities. What has this Venn diagram taught you about your interests?

Remember that note taking is a very personal activity. You've learned a few of the many ways to take notes. What works for you may not work for a friend. And what works for one assignment may not work for another project. Don't be afraid to experiment. You are on your way to becoming a master note taker!

Did you Know this?

Taking good notes is like learning a new sport: it takes patience and practice. It also requires some self-assessment. Reflect on your notes. How would you rate them? Are they very helpful when it's time to study? Maybe you notice that you jot down too many details. It is hard to tell which facts are important. In that case, you should work on learning to tell the difference between important information and extra details. Then you can focus on mainly taking notes on the crucial facts. Learning to evaluate your progress and make changes will not only make you an expert note taker. It is a habit that will serve you well throughout your life.

Glossary

citing **(SITE-ing)** giving credit to the source of a fact, quote, or other information

columns **(KOL-uhmz)** setups of information that run up and down in a chart, table, or on a printed page

flow charts **(FLOH CHARTSS)** diagrams that show how a process progresses and develops, step by step

graphic organizer **(GRAF-ik OR-guh-nye-zur)** a visual representation that helps organize information and show relationships between ideas

headings **(HED-ingz)** words at the top of pages or paragraphs that act as titles

highlighting **(HYE-lite-ing)** marking words with brightly colored ink to make them stand out on the page

note taking **(NOHT TAYK-ing)** the process of writing down or collecting important information and organizing it in a way that is helpful for later use

reliable sources **(ri-LYE-uh-buhl SOR-siz)** well-researched sources of information that are written by experts, have been reviewed by other experts in the field, and are usually current, depending on the topic

rows **(ROHZ)** setups of information that run side to side in a chart or table

self-assessment **(self-uh-SESS-muhnt)** the process of rating your progress, strengths, and weaknesses and determining points that need improvement or changes you can make

Venn diagram **(VEN DYE-uh-gram)** a graph that organizes information using overlapping circles

Find Out More

BOOKS

Gaines, Ann Graham. *Ace Your Research Paper.* Berkeley Heights, NJ: Enslow Publishers, 2009.

Whitney, Brooks. *How to Master the School Universe: Homework, Teachers, Tests, Bullies, and Other Ways to Survive the Classroom.* New York: Scholastic, 2004.

WEB SITES

KidsHealth—Six Steps to Smarter Studying

kidshealth.org/kid/feeling/school/studying.html

This resource offers great study tips, including advice for taking notes.

OSLIS—How to Take GOOD Notes

elementary.oslis.org/research/takenotes/howtotakegoodnotes

Improve your note-taking skills with activities and information from the Oregon School Library Information System.

Scholastic—Venn Diagram

teacher.scholastic.com/lessonplans/graphicorg/pdfs/venndiagram.pdf

Making a Venn diagram? Print out a template here.

Index

About the Author

Julie Green is an elementary media specialist who lives in beautiful Michigan. She loves going on adventures with her siblings, Mary, Emily, and Joey.